A Fair Deal

SHOPPING FOR SOCIAL JUSTICE

KARI JONES

ORCA BOOK PUBLISHERS

Library and Archives Canada Cataloguing in Publication

Jones, Kari, 1966–, author
A fair deal : shopping for social justice / Kari Jones.
(Orca footprints)

Includes bibliographical references and index.
Issued in print and electronic formats.
ISBN 978-1-4598-1043-3 (hardcover).—ISBN 978-1-4598-1044-0 (pdf).—
ISBN 978-1-4598-1045-7 (epub)

1. Social responsibility of business—Juvenile literature. 2. Commerce—
Social aspects—Juvenile literature. 3. Social justice—Juvenile literature.
I. Title. II. Series: Orca footprints

HD60.J663 2017   j174.4   c2017-900829-3
c2017-900830-7

First published in the United States, 2017
Library of Congress Control Number: 2017932487

Summary: This nonfiction book in the Footprints series, illustrated with color photographs throughout, looks at trade from the perspective of making it fair for all people.

Orca Book Publishers is dedicated to preserving the environment and has printed this book on Forest Stewardship Council® certified paper.

Orca Book Publishers gratefully acknowledges the support for its publishing programs provided by the following agencies: the Government of Canada through the Canada Book Fund and the Canada Council for the Arts, and the Province of British Columbia through the BC Arts Council and the Book Publishing Tax Credit.

The authors and publisher have made every effort to ensure that the information in this book was correct at the time of publication. The authors and publisher do not assume any liability for any loss, damage, or disruption caused by errors or omissions. Every effort has been made to trace copyright holders and to obtain their permission for the use of copyright material. The publisher apologizes for any errors or omissions and would be grateful if notified of any corrections that should be incorporated in future reprints or editions of this book.

Cover images by iStock.com, Getty Images
Back cover images (top left to right): iStock.com, iStock.com, Level Ground Trading; (bottom left to right): Level Ground Trading, Getty Images, Shutterstock.com

Edited by Sarah N. Harvey
Design and production by Teresa Bubela and Jenn Playford

ORCA BOOK PUBLISHERS
www.orcabook.com

Printed and bound in Canada.

20 19 18 17 • 4 3 2 1

Fair Trade tea starts on beautiful farms like this one. CHEMC/GETTY IMAGES

To Michael and Rowan

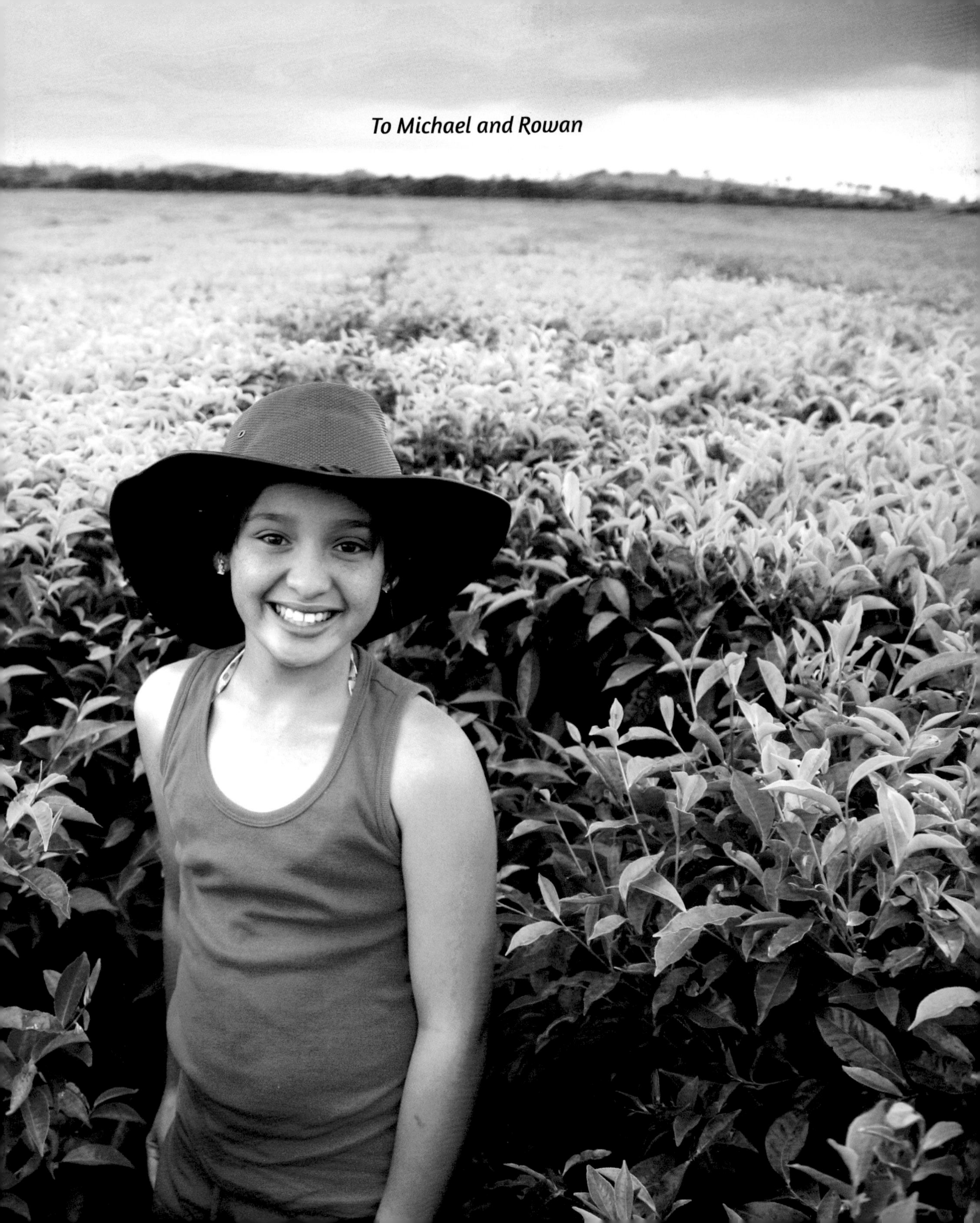

Contents

CHAPTER ONE:
TIME TO TRADE

CHAPTER TWO:
ALL PEOPLE COUNT

CHAPTER THREE:
WHAT FAIR LOOKS LIKE

CHAPTER FOUR:
MAKING CHANGE

Introduction

Mum and me wearing dresses made by women in a Tanzanian cooperative.
MICHAEL PARDY

Do you ever wonder who makes your T-shirts? Or where the melons in your fruit salad are grown? Or how soccer balls get those little stitches in them?

I was always curious about where things came from, but I never thought too much about it until I was in my early twenties and I visited my parents, who were living in Tanzania. My mother and I visited a *cooperative* (a small group of people who all own a business together) where artisans made beautiful wooden toys and hand-sewn clothes. The artisans explained that they used to sell their goods on street corners until they joined the cooperative, but since then they'd had a steady income and were able to sell their goods to people around the world. Speaking to those craftspeople made me realize that

A group of Rwandan artisan women work on a cloth decorated with embroidered patterns. SARINE ARSLANIAN/SHUTTERSTOCK.COM

when we buy things, we are connecting ourselves to a whole web of people across the globe. The idea was exciting, and when I came home to Canada, I joined a group called the Gaia Project, which works with people just like those workers in Tanzania.

Through the Gaia Project, I learned more about how trade works and the effect it has on people's lives. I learned about *sweat shops* and child labor and environmental problems. It turns out that a lot of people work hard to make sure that the folks who grow and make the things we buy get a fair deal. Read on to find out about all these amazing people.

This Zambian girl is collecting palms to make woven baskets for a fair trade project. VIDEA

CHAPTER ONE

Time to Trade

MESSAGE IN A BOTTLE

Have you ever put a message in a bottle and thrown it into the ocean or a river? Did you try to guess who might find it? I wonder if the people who make the things we buy ever think about us. Does a seamstress imagine the person who's going to wear the shirt she made? Do farmers wonder who will eat the spinach they grew? How about you? Do you ever wonder about the people who make your things? Who they are, where they work, where they live, how old they are? These are the questions I asked myself when I started writing this book.

Economists (people who study how trade works) say that trade has three phases.

1. *Production*: when things are grown or made
2. *Distribution*: when things are shipped from farms or factories to stores
3. *Consumption*: when people buy things and eat, drink or use them

This boy found a message in a bottle eight years after it was cast into the sea. He lives in Ireland, and the girls who sent it are from Canada. They were delighted to hear from him!
AOIFE MILLEA/CLEARE PHOTOGRAPHY

CROP TO CUP

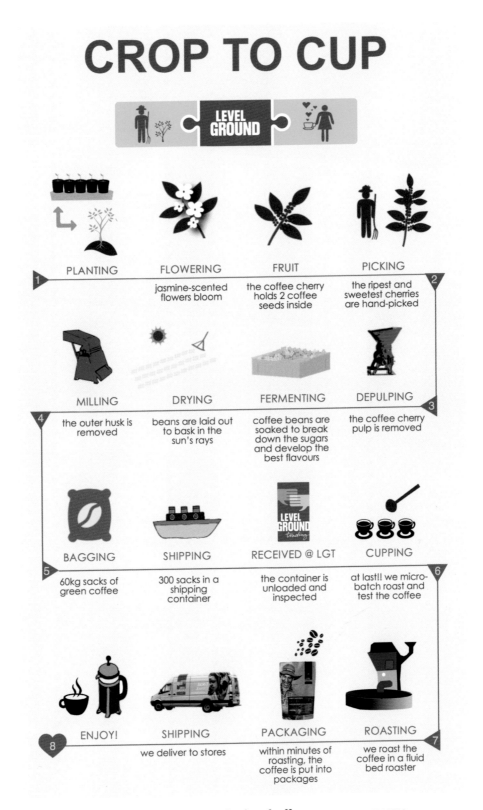

LEVEL GROUND

1 PLANTING | FLOWERING | FRUIT | PICKING **2**

FLOWERING — jasmine-scented flowers bloom

FRUIT — the coffee cherry holds 2 coffee seeds inside

PICKING — the ripest and sweetest cherries are hand-picked

4 MILLING | DRYING | FERMENTING | DEPULPING **3**

MILLING — the outer husk is removed

DRYING — beans are laid out to bask in the sun's rays

FERMENTING — coffee beans are soaked to break down the sugars and develop the best flavours

DEPULPING — the coffee cherry pulp is removed

5 BAGGING | SHIPPING | RECEIVED @ LGT | CUPPING **6**

BAGGING — 60kg sacks of green coffee

SHIPPING — 300 sacks in a shipping container

RECEIVED @ LGT — the container is unloaded and inspected

CUPPING — at last!! we micro-batch roast and test the coffee

8 ENJOY! | SHIPPING | PACKAGING | ROASTING **7**

SHIPPING — we deliver to stores

PACKAGING — within minutes of roasting, the coffee is put into packages

ROASTING — we roast the coffee in a fluid bed roaster

A lot of work goes into the production of coffee. LEVEL GROUND TRADING

People all around the world enjoy shopping at markets where they can meet farmers and eat the freshest fruit and vegetables.
MEINZAHN/SHUTTERSTOCK.COM

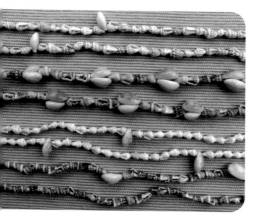

In ancient times, shells like these were used as currency in many parts of the world.
VICKYRU/ISTOCK

Together these phases make up what's called the *supply chain*, which brings us goods from around the world. Studying how the supply chain works helped me answer my questions about where things come from and who makes them.

WILL THAT BE CASH OR COW?

If you go to a farmers' market, you can fill your basket or cloth bag with fruits and vegetables fresh-picked that morning. Where I live, there are markets all over the city. Families from the neighborhood come to buy food and listen to music and hang out with their friends. It's fun, and we often come home with fresh strawberries (my favorite) and vegetables to cook for dinner.

People all around the world have been going to local farmers' markets for thousands of years. As soon as our ancestors started planting and growing crops about 12,000 years ago, they also started having markets. At first, people simply traded what they already had for something they wanted (this system is called *barter*). But barter doesn't always work too well. What if you don't have something the farmer wants in exchange for his cabbages or corn? Pretty soon, people started using money (also called *currency*). Instead of trading one good for another, they paid for what they wanted using things like cattle and grains. Over time, items like cowrie shells and bags of salt were popular currencies, and by around 6,000 years ago, metals like gold were beginning to appear in the marketplace.

There are still lots of farmers' markets, but nowadays we use coins or paper money or plastic cards as our currency. *Phew!* That's much easier to carry than a cow or a bag of gold. In a farmers' market, the supply chain is very simple. Goods go straight from a farmer to a *consumer* (the person who is going to eat, drink or use the produce—you or me). There are no stops along the way.

CROCODILES AHEAD!

As our ancestors settled into villages and towns, trade grew, and the supply chain became more complicated. For example, the town of Aleppo (in modern-day Syria) had a lot of goats but no silk worms. If a person living there wanted to buy silk to weave into fabric for a coat, they couldn't just walk over to China and buy some. Either they had to send someone on a long trip to buy it for them, or the silk had to come to them. That's where the second phase of the supply chain—distribution—came in. By around 4,000 years ago, people who came to be known as merchants were carrying all kinds of goods, from iron tools to woven cloth, to markets in towns far away. Rivers like the Nile in North Africa, the Tigris and Euphrates in the Middle East, the Indus in India and the Yellow in China became major trade routes for these merchants. They braved rapids and crocodiles to get goods to markets in faraway places. Trade was no longer just about exchanging goods between two people who lived near each other. The supply chain was growing.

Though silk originated in China, trade brought it to India, where it became an important part of the culture. WIKIPEDIA.ORG/EDWIN LORD WEEKS

Explorers took to the seas in ships like these and were gone from their families for years at a time. JOHN CLEVELEY/WIKIMEDIA.ORG

For hundreds of years, rivers and oceans were the main trade highways of the world. In fact, it was the possibility of trade that sent the explorers Ferdinand Magellan, James Cook and Francis Drake on voyages around the world, not knowing if they would ever return. They were willing to take the risk because of the riches they might find. It didn't take long before chocolate, sugar, coffee, spices, furs and minerals found their way across oceans and into Europe.

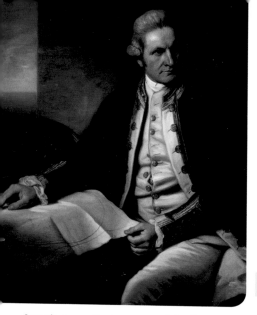

Captain James Cook was one of the first Europeans to sail to North America, Australia and New Zealand.
NATHANIEL DANCE-HOLLAND/WIKIPEDIA.ORG

A CAMEL AT THE DOOR

Trade was so important to our ancestors that some trade routes became famous. Imagine standing in the town center in what is now Istanbul, Turkey, around 2,000 years ago when a caravan came in from the Silk Road carrying goods from faraway China. Long rows of camels would lope into the square, their backs piled high with bags. Imagine the excitement as the camel drivers opened the bags to reveal silks and spices and gold. Maybe, if you were lucky, there'd be a bag of sugar you could stick your finger into.

Even today, camel caravans like this one in Africa's Danakil Desert, Ethiopia, carry goods to faraway places.
FREDY THUERIG/SHUTTERSTOCK.COM

We still have trade routes today. Think of all the cargo ships carrying everything from cell phones to bananas across the seas. Our houses are like the old town centers where the caravans unloaded their wares, only nowadays our things come to us by ship, airplane, train or truck. Imagine what it would be like if a camel carrying bags of groceries or running shoes showed up at your door!

Almost 90 percent of the world's goods are still transported by ship. ROZA/DREAMSTIME.COM

FULL STEAM AHEAD

When the Industrial Revolution started in England in the late 1700s, many people moved from towns and villages into the cities to work for the new steam-powered factories. (To learn more about the Industrial Revolution and its effect on the world, read *Pocket Change*, by Michelle Mulder). Shoppers were happy because the goods made in factories were cheap and easily accessible.

In My Basket

Once, when I was in London, England, I went out for a walk but turned right around and came back inside. The air was so thick with smog that it burned my eyes and made my snot black. My friends told me that before World War II, London air was often like that, because of all the coal fires burning in homes and factories. They called days like that "pea soupers," because the air was so thick. London is better now, but people say that in Beijing, China, the air is so polluted that breathing it does as much damage to the lungs as smoking 40 cigarettes a day.

In this photo from 1952, it's hard to see Nelson's Column in London through the dense smog caused by coal burning.
N T STOBBS/WIKIPEDIA.ORG

It's no coincidence that the first department store, Harding, Howell & Company's Grand Fashionable Magazine, opened in 1796 in London, England. Soon, buying factory-made goods in department stores was the fashionable thing to do.

At first, workers were happy too. They got a steady paycheck, and they could live in the city near schools for their kids. But there were many problems with these steam-powered factories.

DANGER!

Factories were created to make things as quickly and cheaply as possible, so factory owners didn't pay much attention to working conditions. Many factories were dark and smelly and dangerous. People were paid so poorly that sometimes whole families, even the children, had to work to make enough money to eat. In many factories, owners didn't maintain their machines, and there were frequent accidents. Children were often used to repair machines because they were small and could get into

In My Basket

When my son was three, our family spent some time in Guatemala. One day we were hanging out in the park, kicking a soccer ball around, when three eight- or nine-year-old boys came and joined the game. They were really, really good soccer players, and my son was having a blast playing with them. But after a few minutes they said they had to go. Where do you have to go, we asked. Back to work, they said. We kept playing soccer once they had gone, but I was sure glad I wouldn't have to send my young son off to work in a few years.

Kids in Guatemala love to play soccer.
KARI JONES

hard-to-reach and dangerous places. Engine fumes threatened children's lungs, and it was not uncommon for child laborers to become sick. Children were often paid very little, which meant they had to work long hours to make enough money for their family instead of going to school. Most child laborers couldn't even read.

It got so bad by 1802 that England had to introduce the first laws to limit the amount of time a child could work in a factory to twelve hours a day. Can you imagine working that long? It wasn't until the Factory Act of 1833 that a law came into effect banning children under the age of nine from working at all. Finally, in 1847, not even adults were allowed to work more than ten hours at a time. In the United States, it wasn't until 1938 that the Fair Labor Standards Act prohibited children under sixteen years of age from working in manufacturing and mining.

Addie Card was twelve years old when she started working as a spinner in a mill in Vermont. LIBRARY OF CONGRESS/WIKIMEDIA.ORG

Boys working at a glassworks in Indiana in 1908. LEWIS HINE/WIKIMEDIA.ORG

The Great Smog in London in 1952 caused about four thousand people to die. After that smog, regulations were put into place.
MANFREDXY/SHUTTERSTOCK.COM

FEEDING THE FACTORIES

The engines in the new factories could run all day, so they were hungry for more raw materials to make things out of. The more sugar or cocoa or cotton was imported by factory owners from farms and plantations around the world, the more the machines demanded. Factory owners were always on the lookout for the cheapest crops to feed their machines, and if a farmer wouldn't sell crops cheaply enough, the factory owner just went along to the next farmer and bought his or her crops instead. Farmers around the world were feeding the factories, but they weren't making any money. Over time, rich factory owners got richer, and poor farmers got poorer.

The environment was suffering too. Those hungry factory engines needed so much fuel that entire forests were cut down. The factory engines ate the forests and then belched out smoke that hung in the air and made breathing difficult. Waste and used water from these factories were drained into the rivers. In many places around the world, forests, rivers and even the air took a hard hit when the factories got into full swing.

ALL ABOARD!

Steam engines didn't just change the production of goods. They also changed the distribution of them. Rather than having to rely on camels (who can only walk so fast) or sailing ships (which rely on good weather), by the late 1700s, factory owners could send their goods across the world on steam-powered boats and railways. Factory owners used their ships to *import* (bring into the country) raw materials like cotton, cocoa, sugar, coffee, tea, spices, wood and minerals. Their factory workers cooked or wove or shaped the raw materials into food and clothes and

In 1861 there were 30,591 miles of train tracks in the United States.
UGIS RIBA/SHUTTERSTOCK.COM

other products. Then the factory owner would *export* (send out of the country) the finished products. Soon people around the world were sampling goods made in Europe and North America. The supply chain was bigger than it had ever been, but there were a lot of problems with it.

Over the last 200 years we've had what you might call a trade explosion. Now it's almost impossible to imagine a world without the supply chain bringing us things from far away. Nowadays we still have markets and department stores, but we also have online shops, and we can buy things from around the corner or around the world. Markets, department stores and online stores all rely on the supply chain.

MAKING CHANGE

Today, many countries like Canada have laws regulating work and ensuring workers' rights to safety and good wages. But that isn't true everywhere. In the 1980s and '90s, children in Pakistan as young as five or six were working in soccer ball factories and were being paid as little as six cents an hour. In 2013, an unsafe eight-story building in Dhaka, Bangladesh, collapsed, killing 1,134 of the 2,500 garment workers inside. In Guiyu, China, workers dismantle 680,000 kilograms (1.5 million pounds) of junked computers, cell phones and other electronics every year, exposing themselves to toxic waste as they work. None of these people are protected by laws regulating how or where they work.

By the mid-1900s, many people around the world were upset at the way trade was happening. People didn't want to buy soccer balls made by a kid in Pakistan or chocolate from a poor farmer in Peru. It just didn't make sense. Instead, they came up with another system, and they called it Fair Trade.

A boy at work in a textile factory in Delhi, India.
PAUL PRESCOTT/DREAMSTIME.COM

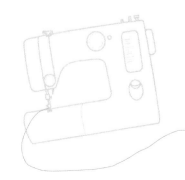

CHAPTER TWO

All People Count

THAT'S NOT FAIR!

Do you ever have to wash the dishes? Or make your bed? How about taking out the garbage (*yuck*)? In many families kids do chores, and every chore a kid does helps the household run more smoothly. Imagine that all the kids in your family did chores, but only one of you got thanked for it. That kid got an allowance, was allowed to stay up later, had more screen time and even got more treats at dinner. That's not fair!

Now imagine that all the kids in your family do chores, and all of your hard work is recognized and appreciated equally. All the kids get a bit of money or privileges, and the kids who do the harder (or more disgusting) chores get a little bit more money and a few more privileges.

That seems fair, doesn't it?

Working together makes the job easier.
LEVEL GROUND TRADING

18

That's what fair trade is like. It's about making sure the work people do is recognized and paid for appropriately. That's called *social justice*, which means treating everyone fairly.

LACE IN THE TRUNK

Fair trade started way back in 1946 when an American woman named Edna Ruth Byler visited a sewing class in Puerto Rico, where she saw women learning how to make beautiful lace. She also saw that they lived in poverty. That didn't make sense. How could they sell such beautiful things, but not be making much money? She bought a lot of lace and took it back home to the United States, where she sold it out of the trunk of her car. After selling lace that way for many years, she started the organization Ten Thousand Villages, which now has stores all across North America and sells fair trade products made in communities all around the world.

Ten Thousand Villages has been helping artisans from all over the world sell their wares since 1946. MARIA LYONS

In fair trade projects, people from different cultures work together. HABIBUL HAQUE/DRIKTEN/TENTHOUSANDVILLAGES.COM

Edna Ruth Byler started a worldwide movement. At first, fair trade projects were mostly run by Christian missionaries (people who travelled to foreign countries to promote their religion). They sold products from the countries where they had missions to members of their churches in North America. It wasn't until the 1960s and '70s that fair trade stores started up.

During that time, there were so many people saying they were selling fair trade goods that it got very confusing, and shoppers didn't have any way of knowing if what they bought was really fairly traded or not. Imagine walking into a store and buying a toy for a friend. If the shopkeeper told you it was a fair trade toy, how would you know what that meant, or if the storekeeper was telling you the truth? Many consumers had exactly that problem. Finally, in 1988, a Dutch organization called Max Havelaar came up with some standards so that people would know whether something was truly fair trade. Now there are organizations that keep track of fair trade projects, and we know that if something has a fair trade label on it, it was made using the fair trade principles.

Hugo Ciro from Level Ground Trading working on a coffee farm. LEVEL GROUND TRADING

HOW DOES IT WORK?

Like any kind of trade, fair trade relies on the supply chain. The difference is that in fair trade, all the people along the chain are treated with respect. That means they have the opportunity to make a good wage, work in clean and safe environments, and have their culture and traditions valued.

Fair trade projects often start when people in one country have some connection to people in another country. That's what happened to Hugo Ciro. Hugo lives in Victoria, British Columbia, but he grew up in Colombia. As a child, he often visited his grandparents' coffee farm in the mountains of Antioquia, Colombia. It was a very poor region. When Hugo moved to Canada, he and some friends started Level Ground

In Ethiopia, a lot of the work takes place outside, including drying coffee beans. LEVEL GROUND TRADING

In My Basket

One day when we were in Guatemala, we went to visit a fair trade coffee cooperative. It was beautiful there, and the people had nice houses with yards full of flowers and vegetables. They told us that before they became a cooperative, they were so poor they couldn't always feed their children, even though they lived on a farm. Ever since then, I have always made sure to buy fair trade coffee. I don't drink coffee often, but when I do, I think of those flower gardens on the coffee farm in Guatemala.

I do enjoy a good cup of fair trade coffee.
KARI JONES

Fair trade projects are good for everyone, from young to old. LEVEL GROUND TRADING

Trading—and his first trading partners were the coffee growers of Antioquia. Level Ground Trading is based in Victoria, but it has grown so much that now it has partners in Colombia, Bolivia, Peru, Ethiopia, Tanzania and the Philippines.

GETTING STARTED

Figuring out how to create a fair wage for everyone is one of the first things any fair trade project does. If people are working for low wages in an unsafe factory, or if they are not getting paid well for their crops, then the supply chain they are part of is not fair.

Imagine a farmer in Bolivia who grows cacao beans for chocolate. He wants to sell his beans for a good price so he can provide for his family. Business is tough, though, because he is competing with all the other cacao farmers in the area. Prices are low and not steady. He is not sure he should stay in business. *Hmm…*doesn't sound great, does it?

After much thought, he decides to get together with the other farmers in the area and start a cooperative. Cooperatives, or co-ops, are small groups of people who all own a business together.

Level Ground owners visit one of the cooperative farms in Colombia. LEVEL GROUND TRADING

When farmers cooperate, they can demand a better price for their crops and have a better income to support their families.

FLUSH WITH MONEY...

Fair trade projects are often made up of cooperatives of farmers who band together to help each other out. They usually have someone who works for them make sure that the crops they are selling are of the best quality and that the farmers get a good price for their crops. Fair trade partners usually buy the crops for a little bit more than the market price (the price most farmers are selling that crop for). Some of the extra money gets put into a community fund, which the community decides how to spend.

For example, the Makaibari Tea Estate in Darjeeling, India, in the foothills of the Himalayas, is home to over 800 workers living in seven villages on the estate. The extra cash they get from their fair trade partnership is used to benefit the whole community. Girls can train to become midwives to help mothers and their newborn babies. The community also built a library with new computers, and all of the villages on the tea estate have electricity and flush toilets.

UNITED WE STAND

It's not just farmers who start cooperatives and fair trade projects. Factory workers do too. For example, in Thanapara Swallows, near the Ganges River in northwest Bangladesh, over 200 women dye and weave yarns into fabrics, which are then embroidered and tailored into clothing. The factory was started after many men in the village were killed in 1971 during the War of Independence (also known as the Liberation War). Women suddenly had to make money to take care of their families, but all they knew how to do was sew and make clothing.

Tea is picked by hand, then carried in baskets to a central sorting area. T PHOTOGRAPHY/SHUTTERSTOCK.COM

The factory gave them an opportunity to make a good living, and it even has a fund that sends over 300 kids to school. The Rajlakshmi Cotton Mills in Delhi, India, is another good example, because it ensures that fair trade is practiced throughout the supply chain right down to the cotton farmers. These factories are a far cry from the dirty, dangerous cotton factories of the Industrial Revolution!

READY FOR SCHOOL

Farmers and factory workers around the world understand how important education is. They want their kids to have opportunities to follow their dreams and passions. As a result, community funds are often spent on education for the kids of the community. That's what happened to Martin. When he was a child, he lived on a coffee farm near a small town called Andes, in central Colombia. He wanted to go to high school but didn't have money to buy shoes, so he sold peanuts at the mall. One day he heard about Famicafé, a fair trade cooperative that had scholarships to help kids go to school. Martin told his parents about it, and they joined Famicafé. Martin went all the way through school, and now he works as a veterinarian, helping take care of the cooperative's animals.

Famicafé has granted over a thousand scholarships to send Colombian farmers' kids to school. LEVEL GROUND TRADING

Sometimes money is spent on simpler things. In Colombia, the same cooperative that Martin belongs to helps a rural school in the area keep its fields fenced. Why? So that cows don't come in and break the bamboo piping that brings water to the school. Fences really do make good neighbors.

DON'T THROW THAT AWAY

Respecting culture is an important part of fair trade partnerships. Many people around the world produce traditional arts and crafts, and a lot of fair trade projects help workers use their traditions

to make a living. In Escama Studio, Brazilian women crochet metal pull tabs into handcrafts that look like they're made from fish scales. Brazilians traditionally used crochet as an inexpensive way to create clothing and other items. Now women use modern materials instead of wool to make tops and bracelets and handbags. I bet you never knew soda can tabs could be so beautiful.

Many of the women work at home, allowing them to be near their children, which preserves another important piece of their traditional culture.

LIVING LANDSCAPES

Taking care of the environment is usually one of the top things communities want to do with the help of their fair trade partnership. What good is being a farmer if the land you want to farm is eroded or polluted, or if the water you need for your crops is full of chemicals?

In an area of the Philippines called Cordilleras, people have been growing rice for centuries on the sides of the mountains. They stop it from sliding down the mountain by making terraces—low, flat "patios" made of soil and water. In 1995 the United Nations declared the area to be a UNESCO World Heritage "cultural living landscape" because it is so beautiful, and because rice is so important to the people who live there.

This system had been working for centuries, but the land wasn't producing much rice anymore because of environmental problems like contaminated water. Many farmers had to leave their farms and move to the cities, and the people who stayed were very poor.

A fair trade project called RICE Inc. (which stands for Revitalizing Indigenous Cordillera Entrepreneurs) started helping the farmers grow *heritage strains* of rice that have existed for centuries. These heritage strains grew so well that the farmers didn't have to use the harmful chemicals anymore,

Ivone crochets soda-can tabs into beautiful items for Escama Studio in Brazil.
ESCAMASTUDIO

Though the Philippines is a small country, it is one of the largest rice producers in the world.
SUC/ISTOCK.COM

Heritage rice comes in different sizes and colors. KARI JONES

and their terraces were saved. In fact, this rice grows so well that during harvest, the ground all around the farmers' houses is covered in drying rice, and some families are making enough money they can put some savings aside. I can buy heritage Philippine rice in the supermarket near my home. Some of it is black, some red and some pink. It's delicious.

LET'S PLAY!

Kids should be at school or at play, not at work. That is one of the key beliefs of all fair trade projects. I mentioned in Chapter One that in the 1990s, kids as young as five or six were working in factories stitching soccer balls. In 1996, the International Labour Organization estimated that there were more than 7,000 children between the ages of five and fourteen working full-time stitching soccer balls in Pakistan, where most of the world's soccer balls come from. Factory owners hired children because they have good eyesight and their hands are small, so they can make those tiny stitches. Doesn't that sound like something a factory owner in the Industrial Revolution would do?

FIFA estimates that 265 million people play soccer worldwide. That's a lot of soccer balls being kicked around.
SNEHAL JEEVAN PAILKAR/SHUTTERSTOCK.COM

Talon Sports in Pakistan decided they wanted to make a change. Since 2002 they have stopped using children to stitch their sports balls, and now they have a factory where adults can work in clean, well-lit spaces and make enough money that their kids don't have to work. Fair trade projects in Pakistan have paid for communities to get clean drinking water, access to health care, daycare facilities and even bicycles to help people get to and from work more easily. And, of course, they send kids to school.

MAKING IT FAIR

All these fair trade projects protect the people and environments along the supply chain. That means when we buy fair trade items, we can be sure that the factory or farm where they were made didn't use child labor, it paid its workers well, it respected the environment where the people live, and it helped people keep their cultural traditions alive.

FAIR TRADE FACT:
What do all of these things have in common: Coffee, tea, herbs, cocoa, fresh fruit and vegetables, sugar, beans, grains, flowers, nuts, oils, butters, honey, spices, wine, seafood, clothing, body care products, gold, precious metals, diamonds, handcrafts and sports balls? They can all be found with a fair trade label on them.

In My Basket

In Guatemala, we met a woman who always sat under a tree near our language school and wove beautiful cloth. We thought it was ingenious how she wrapped a strap around her hips at one end and a tree at the other, and made herself into a living loom. One day she told us she was using a traditional Guatemalan weaving technique, and she asked me if I wanted to try. She helped me make myself into a loom, but my weaving was pretty messy, and soon I had to hand it back. We all had a good laugh over my weaving efforts.

Weaving is much harder than it looks.
KARI JONES

CHAPTER THREE

What Fair Looks Like

HOW DOES IT ALL WORK?

Women in India explain how their bags are made. RYAN JACOBS/TENTHOUSANDVILLAGES.COM

What if all shoes were made in the same size? That wouldn't work, would it? My son's feet are so big I can grow plants in his shoes, but my nephew is only six, so his feet are tiny. There's no way they could swap shoes.

Trade is like that too. What works for one group of people doesn't work for another. Imagine having the same rules for cacao farmers and basket weavers. Doesn't make sense, does it? Every project has its own way of working.

Even though fair trade projects come in different shapes and sizes, there are some things that always stay the same. There are always producers—the farmers or factory workers who make the products. They're the first people on the supply chain. There are always the business people living in places like Canada, the United States, Europe and Australia who buy goods from the producers and sell them in stores and online. They are the second group of people on the supply chain. And there are always the buyers—people like you and me. We are the end of the supply chain.

SOMETIMES IT'S BIG

A large fair trade project is like a big ant colony. Have you ever been to a bug zoo and seen an ant colony in action? You know the kind I mean, with tunnels leading away from a central hub to smaller hubs farther away? That's what a large fair trade organization is like. The faraway hubs are the farms, and the central hub is the cooperative where all their goods end up.

WORMS FOR SALE!

Can you imagine sticking your hand in a tree branch and gathering a whole pile of sticky worm cocoons? That's what the silk farmers in Ethiopia do. They farm worms. It sounds strange, but it's not. Did you know when you wear silk you're wearing

FAIR TRADE FACT:
About 85 percent of the world's farms are still less than 2 hectares in size. That's about twice the size of most soccer fields. Those small farms grow about 70 percent of the world's food.

Producers grow, harvest, sort and prepare crops before they pass them along to distributors. LEVEL GROUND TRADING

a worm's home? Really. Silk is made from the cocoons that silk worms spin so that they can grow into moths.

Worm cocoons are made out of long strands of silk that can be spun and woven into cloth, then dyed any color of the rainbow. People around the world pay a lot of money to wear silk, and it all starts on small farms in places like Ethiopia.

Sabahar is a company that makes silk and cotton clothes. It is a fair trade company that works with farmers throughout Ethiopia. It buys silk from small, rural farms, then hires spinners and weavers to make it into cloth. Some of the spinners and weavers work at the Sabahar factory, and some work at home. In Ethiopia the women spin the fibers into skeins of silk, and the men weave that into fabric.

Once the fibers are spun into silk threads, they need to be dyed. Sabahar uses flowers, coffee grounds, bark, roots and even insects to make these threads colorful. All this is done in their factory by artists. Then the colorful threads are woven into cloth

A woman shows off a piece of cloth that will be sold through Sabahar in Ethiopia.
JONI KABANA/SABAHAR

In My Basket

The year I was twenty-six, my family and I spent some time in northern Jamaica where we visited a farmers' cooperative. Being Canadians, we were used to farms that stretched for miles and miles, so we were surprised at how small these farms were, but when the farmers showed us what they were growing, we were amazed. On their small plots they grew cassava and yams in the ground, peppers and beans and leafy greens on top of the ground, and papayas and mangoes in the trees. Those small farms sure produced a lot of food! One of the farmers gave us a mango to share. Yum! That was one delicious piece of fruit.

My family learned a lot about crops when visiting this farm in Jamaica.
KARI JONES

Awash cotton towels made by spinners at Sabahar work perfectly as cover ups after a swim. SOPHIE JOY MOSKO/SABAHAR

and prepared for sale. So if you are wearing something made out of silk, you might be wearing worm homes and coffee grounds.

Sabahar is one of those big fair trade projects that's like an ant colony, with all the farmers bringing their silk to the central hub.

SOMETIMES IT TAKES A VILLAGE

Sometimes things that look easy are actually hard to do. Weaving is one of those things. In Lyamutinga in western Zambia, making woven baskets takes a whole village. First, the kids go out and gather leaves from palm trees and roots of a local plant called *mukenge*. Then they help their mothers scrape the fibers into long threads that can be woven. While the men and women weave the baskets, their children and babies watch them. That way the families can stay together, and the kids can learn the craft.

The villagers of Lyamutinga worked this way for centuries, but in recent years kids stopped wanting to help out because no one was buying the baskets anymore. That's where the fair trade partnership came in. In 2007, some Canadians from an organization called the Victoria International Development Agency (VIDEA) stopped by their village and admired the baskets so much that they decided to start a fair trade project. Now kids are happy to gather roots and be part of the process, because the money the community makes from the baskets helps pay their school fees.

MEBELO'S FAMILY

Kebby Lingomba Mandandi is a basket weaver and father of six children. Kebby didn't go to school, so finding work was hard, and their family was poor. But then Kebby started weaving baskets for the fair trade project in his community. With the money he made from his work he was able to send the eldest

Kebby Lingomba Mandandi weaves a basket.
VIDEA

three kids to school. His eldest daughter is now a police officer in the Republic of Zambia.

Kebby's third child, Mebelo, completed grade 12 in 2015 at Muoyo Secondary School. She had to travel five and a half kilometers to get to school, but she did it every day. She did well in school and will definitely go to college. Mebelo says, "All this achievement is attributed to my father, who managed to pay for my school fees because he is a basket weaver who sells baskets to VIDEA in Canada. I am happy for him being a basket weaver because without him selling baskets, I was going to stay home."

Mebelo Mandandi. VIDEA

SOMETIMES IT'S LITTLE

Not all farmers or craftspeople are able to join a co-op. Sometimes they live too far away from other people. Sometimes there isn't anyone else making the same craft. In that case, the farmer or artisan has to sell directly to a fair trade partner.

In Nairobi, Kenya, there are a lot of people living in deep poverty. They don't have money, they don't have farms or factories, but they do have skills, and they have imagination. Lizzi is a designer and artist who makes bracelets and necklaces out of beads. One day, someone asked Lizzi for food, but she saw that what he really needed was a way to make a better life for himself. So she asked him to gather all the plastic bags lying around the streets, and she showed him how to make soccer balls out of plastic bags. He started selling plastic soccer balls and was able to make enough money to buy himself food. Now he and Lizzi work together making bracelets and, of course, soccer balls. Their bracelets are sold through a fair trade distributor in Canada. Lizzi is not part of a fair trade co-op, and sometimes people call this type of fair trade "direct trade" because the goods go directly from the person who makes them to the person who sells them to us.

Baskets are used all over the world, including in Vietnam, where they are used in floating markets.
QUANGPRAHA/ISTOCK.COM

In My Basket

My mother and I really love baskets, so when we visited a wheat farm in western Tanzania some years ago, we were delighted to see beautiful woven baskets all over the place. While my father and husband went to talk to the farmers about the wheat, my mother and I talked to the women about the baskets. We sat and drank tea, and they showed us how they made them. I still have the baskets we bought from those women, and every time I see them I think about how friendly they were and how talented!

Even years later these baskets from Tanzania brighten up our home. KARI JONES

MAKING DREAMS COME TRUE

Many people turn to fair trade projects to make their dreams come true. In many places around the world, it's hard for people with disabilities to get jobs, especially people in wheelchairs. In Cambodia, an organization called VillageWorks employs young people with physical handicaps to sew and tailor. Recently they changed their whole workshop so that people in wheelchairs can move around more easily.

GETTING IT OUT THERE

We've seen a lot of examples of the production end of the supply chain, but what about the next step along the way—the distribution phase? This is another place where "one size fits all" doesn't work.

A large fair trade organization like Level Ground Trading (from Chapter Two) has a lot of people involved in distribution. There are the people who go to other countries to test and taste the goods. (The ones who taste chocolate are the luckiest.) They negotiate with the co-ops to set a fair price, and they also spend time getting to know the people they are buying from. Then, back at home, there are the salespeople, who convince grocery stores and other shops to sell their fair trade goods, and there are the people who get the fair trade products to the shops and grocery stores on time. Then there are the financial people who make sure the money goes to the places it needs to go to, and the marketing people who create the advertisements, and…*phew*… so many people.

For some smaller projects, the whole thing is much simpler because the person buying the goods will also sell them at fairs and online. That's how it works for the basket weavers of Lyamutinga. Each year they sell the baskets they weave to their fair trade partners in Canada at VIDEA, who sell them directly to consumers at a fair trade fair and online through their website.

Kids in Zambia prepare materials for making woven baskets. KARI JONES

CHAPTER FOUR

Making Change

The final part of the fair trade supply chain is the buyers. That's you and me!

CHANGING THE WORLD

How many people in the world are you connected to? It's hard to answer that question, but one way to do it is to take a look inside your closet. Most clothing labels indicate where the item is made. What story do your clothes tell you? If you could put pins in a map of the world to show all the places your clothing comes from, how many pins would there be?

I teach at a college, and at the beginning of every school year I like to buy one or two new pieces of clothing. It feels good to start the year with a new shirt or sweater. If you need new clothes because you've grown and there isn't anything in your family's closets that fits you, take a look and see if there is a place nearby or online where you can buy fair trade clothing. Sometimes it is a bit more expensive, but it's worth it to know you have helped someone have a better life!

Check the labels of your clothes to see how many places you are connected to.
BROOKE BECKER/SHUTTERSTOCK.COM

Fair trade goods from Uganda, brought back directly from the makers to Victoria, BC. JOANNE SPECHT

PSSST...PASS IT ON

Once you've found a place to buy your new fair trade clothes, take a picture of them or of the shop. Ask your parents if you can post it on social media for your friends to see. Maybe they will be inspired to buy fair trade clothing too.

Spreading the word is an important way to help the fair trade movement grow, and there are many ways to do it. You could create a fair trade float for a local parade or set up a fair trade stall at your local market. You could write a paragraph about fair trade in your school newsletter or create a fair trade poster to hang up in your classroom. One group of high school kids in Montclair, New Jersey, started a fair trade caroling group at Christmas. Yes, they were singing for fair trade. Instead of wishing everyone a Merry Christmas, they wished them a Fair Trade Christmas. Passersby heard the songs and stopped to ask questions. The kids were able to spread the word about fair trade—and have fun doing it.

Colorful baskets brighten up store shelves.
JOANNE SPECHT

Different fair trade organizations have different labels, but they all have the words **fair trade** *on them.*
FAIRTRADE CANADA

FAIR TRADE FACT:
Grocery stores in North America sell more bananas than any other fruit.

Avery Jane makes her own skin and hair products using fair trade items. JULIE PAUL

FINDING FAIRNESS

Fair trade organizations make it easy to recognize when you are buying fair trade products. They put labels on clothes, food and anything else they are selling to tell us that the product we are about to buy has been recognized as being fairly traded. Look for these logos to help guide you in your shopping. You can also get fair trade stickers from shops like Ten Thousand Villages or other fair trade stores in your town and attach them to your backpack or bike or skateboard. That's another way to let other people know about fair trade.

CUPCAKES FOR SALE!

There are a lot of ways you can make your own household more fair trade–friendly. Avery Jane from Victoria, British Columbia, has always been crafty. When she was ten, she started making her own hair and skin creams. She and her mom bought fair trade Shea butter, beeswax and cocoa butter, and she mixed them together, added tangerine, lavender and vanilla scents to make them smell lovely, and created her own homemade creams. "I wanted to find fair trade products because I wanted to make sure other people weren't suffering," she says.

Now that Avery is a teenager, she also makes yummy cupcakes using fair trade cocoa and coconut oil along with her other ingredients. If you like to bake or do crafts, you can look through your ingredients list to see if there is anything that you could buy fair trade.

Do you ever have bake sales to raise money for sports events or field trips? Ask families who are baking if they can include one or two fair trade ingredients in their baked goods. And if your family goes to a potluck dinner, you might be able to add fair trade ingredients to the food that you take.

HOLIDAYS AND SUMMER FUN

There are so many ways you can use fair trade products in your everyday life. Do you like to camp? There's nothing so wonderful as food cooked over an open fire, especially s'mores, which are made by squishing marshmallows and chocolate between graham crackers and roasting them over the fire. The more chocolate the better, and if it's fair trade chocolate, that's the best.

Chocolate is one of the easiest treats to buy fair trade, and one of the yummiest too. In North America we eat a lot of chocolate, especially at Easter. In fact, in North America, people buy more chocolate at Easter than at any other time of year. Does your family or school or church hold an Easter egg hunt? If they do, ask them to use fair trade Easter eggs. (And if they don't have an Easter egg hunt, now's a great time to start. More chocolate for you!) If you celebrate Passover, you can include a wish to end slavery and child labor in cocoa farming as part of your Passover Seder Haggadah. The organization Global Exchange even has a Passover Seder Haggadah insert to help.

Look for fair trade ingredients in the baking section of your local grocery store.
JENS LANGEN/DIVINE CHOCOLATE/TENTHOUSANDVILLAGES.COM

In My Basket

One day when I went grocery shopping, I tried an experiment. Every time I put something in my cart, I looked at where it came from and whether it was fair trade. I was surprised at how many items in my cart came from faraway places like Chile and Israel and India. Not much of my shopping was fair trade, so I decided that each time I shopped, I would try to replace one item with a fair trade equivalent. So far it's going well. I've found fair trade bananas and rice, but I'm still looking for fair trade mangoes.

These are some of the fair trade foods that I found in my pantry.
KARI JONES

About 40 percent of the world's sugar is made from sugar cane, mostly from Fiji, Belize, Paraguay, Mauritius and Jamaica. LEVEL GROUND TRADING

Easter and Passover aren't the only holidays when you can make fair trade choices. At Halloween you can ask your parents to help you make treats from fair trade chocolate and sugar to hand out, and on Valentine's Day your classmates or teacher might like the same treats. Any time you and your family share feasts and treats, try to include some fair trade products.

IT'S A CHALLENGE

In 2016, the Girl Guides of the Prairie Rose area of Alberta held a chocolate challenge to learn all about fair trade chocolate. First, they talked about where chocolate comes from and who makes it. They learned why it's important to buy fair trade chocolate and what logos to look for when they're choosing their chocolate treats. Then they played games like Chocolate Bingo, and finally they made and ate chocolate treats. Now that's what I call a great challenge.

If you belong to a club or sports team, or if your family belongs to a church, temple or mosque, ask your leaders if you can have a "fair trade day." People would learn all about fair trade and play games, just like the Girl Guides in Alberta.

FAIR TRADE SCHOOLS

Schools across North America and Europe are going fair trade. That means they have clubs that encourage students and their families to learn about fair trade. They also strive to use fair trade ingredients in their cafeterias and bake sales.

Media Elementary School in Pennsylvania was one of the first in the United States to become a fair trade school. They started with students in the grade five class, who decided to become cocoa farmers for a day and learn what it's like to grow cocoa. The class saw how hard the farmers work and decided they wanted to do something to help those farmers out.

Ninety percent of the world's cocoa is grown on small family farms by about six million farmers, so buying fair trade cocoa has a big impact. HAAK78/SHUTTERSTOCK.COM

Dressing up as a giant banana is one way to raise awareness of fair trade!
FAIRTRADE CANADA

They started a fair trade club, and when their school has a bake sale now, they use at least two fair trade ingredients in their baking. That way everybody remembers the people who grow the spices and sugars we use in our baking. (Plus everyone gets to eat chocolate. That's always a good thing.)

Any school can have a fair trade club. In England, over 1,000 schools have joined the Fairtrade Foundation, and all the kids are learning about their fair trade breakfast. Each school will organize a breakfast where everyone eats fair trade food. Just imagine if they all eat fair trade bananas. That's a whole lot of banana peels! I hope nobody slips.

A fair trade club at your school can do a lot of things. Does your school have a cafeteria, and does it sell fair trade food? If it doesn't, do some research and find out what fair trade food is available in your town that could be sold in the cafeteria.

In My Basket

One day when I was putting away the laundry, I noticed a tag at the back of one of my shirts. It said Made in Mexico. That made me wonder, Where does the rest of my clothing come from? I dug around in my cupboards for a while, and this is the list I came up with. My family's clothing is made in India, China, Mexico, Thailand, Honduras, Taiwan, Dominican Republic, Portugal, Bangladesh, Guatemala, Vietnam, El Salvador, Haiti, Indonesia, Philippines, Hong Kong, Ecuador, Romania, Canada and the United States. We're linked to a lot of people around the world, but how many of them are treated fairly?

Labels on the clothing in my cupboard.
KARI JONES

42

If you're interested in making your school a fair trade school, ask a teacher to help you contact www.fairtradecampaigns.org for support.

HEAR YE, HEAR YE!

Any group of people can go fair trade, even a whole town. And kids like the 2nd New Quay and Llanarth Scouts in Aberaeron, Wales, can help. The kids surveyed forty shops and found that only nine were selling fair trade products. Ten others said they were interested in doing so. Aberaeron later became the one thousandth fair trade town in the United Kingdom.

BE DEMANDING

Telling people what you think is one of the most important ways to make trade fair. If you have a favorite store where your family buys clothes or groceries, ask your parents if you can find their Facebook page and write on it to tell the store that you'd like them to carry fair trade alternatives.

Many years ago Global Exchange started a campaign asking people to write a letter to Starbucks demanding it carry fair trade coffee. So many people wrote letters that Starbucks changed its practices. Now Starbucks is one of the biggest sellers of fair trade coffee in North America. All because people wrote to the company.

SOCCER MANIA

Rowan Nicholas started playing soccer when he was three. By the time he was thirteen, he was on a soccer field four times a week and playing in a competitive league. Soccer was important to him! In the space of a week his foot touched a soccer ball dozens of times. That's why he was excited when he learned

The best way to get local stores to sell fair trade products is to ask the owners to carry them.
TATJANA SPLICHAL/SHUTTERSTOCK.COM

FAIR TRADE FACT:
In April 2000, Garstang in Lancashire, England, declared itself "the World's first Fairtrade Town."

Rowan Nicholas playing soccer.
KARI JONES

about fair trade soccer balls. First he asked his parents for a fair trade soccer ball for Christmas, and then he saved up his allowance and used it to help pay for a fair trade soccer ball for his best friend when his was bitten by a dog and ruined. They took their fair trade soccer balls to practice, and soon the other kids on the team were asking about them. "I love playing soccer, but I don't want kids to make my soccer balls. They should be playing soccer too, not working," Rowan says. When Rowan's little cousin started playing soccer at school, guess what Rowan sent him? A mini fair trade soccer ball!

BUY FAIR, BUY LESS

Fair trade is not about spending more money or buying more stuff. It's about bringing justice to people around the world. Fair trade projects are based on the idea that people need to protect their environments, their families and their homes. Parents want their kids to have the best life they can have. That means they go to school, have access to medicine and doctors, have clean water to drink and good food to eat, and have time to play.

You don't have to spend money to support fair trade. Supporting fair trade is really about making wise choices. A kid who hands out a fair trade flyer or sings a fair trade carol is making as much of a difference as a kid who buys a fair trade T-shirt.

Fair trade is about remembering that we are all connected, and it's about making the connections we have with people around the world as fair as possible.

If you have other ideas for how to get involved with a fair trade project, tell your friends and pass it on. The more people who think about making the supply chain fair, the better.

Fair trade is about keeping families happy and healthy. LEVEL GROUND TRADING

Fair trade dolls. JOANNE SPECHT

Acknowledgments

When I was asked to write a book about fair trade, the first thing I thought was that I would ask Stacey Toews and Hugo Ciro from Level Ground Trading here in Victoria for help. Not only did they offer me a lot of time, but they patiently explained complex ideas so that I could understand them. Many of the beautiful photos in the book come from them, and without them this book would not have been written. Mary Weston from VIDEA sent messages all the way to Zambia on my behalf so that I could hear the voices of people who are directly affected by fair trade. Jacqueline McAdam of Resilient Solutions explained different forms of fair trade to me, from small to very large. Susan Albion of the Global Village Store shared many names with me. James Milligan of Social Conscience Company, Mariana Lamaison Sears from Media, Pennsylvania, and Scott Runkel and Katie Feldman of Cutthroats for Fair Trade, all gave me their time, though they didn't even know me. Thank you all, your generosity was so inspiring.

I'd also like to thank Michelle Mulder, who shared her wisdom about writing informational books, and Sarah Harvey, who guided me with her usual clarity. Julie and Avery Paul, thank you for sharing your story. Alexis Martfeld and Caleb Schulz, thanks to both of you for reading portions of the manuscript.

My writing friends, Laurie Elmquist, Julie Paul, Alisa Gordaneer, Robin Stevenson and Alex Van Tol, all listened with patience. Thanks to Michael Pardy for going over the manuscript with me, and to Dawn Jones for your eagle eye.

Resources

Print

Hess, Ingrid. *Think Fair Trade First!* Indianapolis: Global Gifts, 2010.

Smith, David J. *If the World Were a Village.* Toronto: Kids Can Press, 2011.

Online

If you want to learn more about fair trade and how it works:

Fairtrade International: www.fairtrade.net

Global Exchange fair trade program: www.globalexchange.org/programs/fairtrade

Ten Thousand Villages: www.tenthousandvillages.ca

If you want information on how to start your own fair trade campaign:

Fair Trade Campaigns: www.fairtradecampaigns.org

Glossary

barter—to exchange goods or services without using money

consumer—the person who is going to eat, drink or use a product

consumption—when people buy and use goods; the third and last part of the supply chain

cooperative—an organization, such as a farm, that is owned and run jointly by its members, who share the profits and benefits

currency—the system of money people use within a country

distribution—when goods are shipped from where they are made to where they are sold

economists—the people who study how the economy works; they track how and where goods are produced, distributed and consumed

export—sending goods to another country to be sold

heritage strains—strains of crops that have been around for a long time and have not been modified by humans

import—bringing goods into a country to sell

market price—the price a good sells for in the market; this price usually reflects what most people are willing to pay for that good

production—when goods are made or crops grown; the first step on the supply chain

social justice—when people around the world have equal access to wealth, opportunities and privileges

supply chain—the system that takes goods from the farmer or artisan who grew or made them all the way to the people who buy from the shop

sweat shops—factories or workshops, especially in the clothing industry, where laborers are paid low wages and work long hours under poor conditions

Index

Index (continued)

48